BRANDING
FOR
SUCCESS

A roadmap for raising the visibility & value of your nonprofit organization

By
Larry Checco

USA ▪ Canada ▪ UK ▪ Ireland

Cover illustration by Felix Morales
Original cover concept by Brian Checco

Note for Librarians: a cataloguing record for this book that includes Dewey Decimal Classification and US Library of Congress numbers is available from the Library and Archives of Canada. The complete cataloguing record can be obtained from their online database at:
www.collectionscanada.ca/amicus/index-e.html
ISBN 1-4120-5249-1

TRAFFORD

Offices in Canada, USA, Ireland, UK and Spain

This book was published on-demand in cooperation with Trafford Publishing. On-demand publishing is a unique process and service of making a book available for retail sale to the public taking advantage of on-demand manufacturing and Internet marketing. On-demand publishing includes promotions, retail sales, manufacturing, order fulfilment, accounting and collecting royalties on behalf of the author.

Book sales for North America and international:
Trafford Publishing, 6E–2333 Government St.,
Victoria, BC v8t 4p4 CANADA
phone 250 383 6864 (toll-free 1 888 232 4444)
fax 250 383 6804; email to orders@trafford.com

Book sales in Europe:
Trafford Publishing (uk) Ltd., Enterprise House, Wistaston Road Business Centre,
Wistaston Road, Crewe, Cheshire cw2 7rp UNITED KINGDOM
phone 01270 251 396 (local rate 0845 230 9601)
facsimile 01270 254 983; orders.uk@trafford.com

Order online at:
www.trafford.com/robots/05-0144.html

10 9 8 7 6 5 4 3

This book is dedicated to my family and friends, and to everyone committed to making the world a better place.

Table of Contents

Preface

This book is meant to be a quick, easy—and useful—read.

My 20-plus years of working as a consultant to the nonprofit world have sensitized me to the fact that those to whom this book is directed—namely executive directors, board members, and staff of small- and medium-size organizations—are often overwhelmed by day-to-day operational activities. I felt that a dense tome on branding would be one more book to collect dust on a busy person's shelf.

Instead, the goal was to produce something that could be read in one or two sittings—in an evening or over the course of a weekend, perhaps—and have you, the reader, put it down and say, *"Yes, I can do this!"*

There is nothing in this book that is beyond the reach of any organization, regardless of size or financial resources. Its two primary objectives are: (1) to make the case for branding and its importance to the sustainability—and perhaps even the survivability—of your organization; and (2) to make the fundamental principles of good branding accessible to everyone.

At the same time, it is not meant to be the definitive work on branding. On the contrary, if asked, I'm sure other professionals would offer other approaches. My focus here is to make branding as simple, practical, and cost-effective as possible.

I hope *Branding for Success* motivates and inspires you to raise the visibility and value of your organization. At the very least I hope it puts you in a whole new mindset about how and what to communicate to your audiences, especially when it comes to letting them know who you are, what you do—and why they should care!

Larry Checco

Silver Spring, Maryland

2005

To laugh often and much; to win the respect of intelligent people and the affection of children; to earn the appreciation of honest critics and endure the betrayal of false friends; to appreciate beauty; to find the best in others; to leave the world a bit better, whether by a healthy child, a garden patch, or a redeemed social condition; to know even one life has breathed easier because you have lived; this is to have succeeded.

Ralph Waldo Emerson

The Power of the Brand

When people see your organization's name and logo, do they truly understand who you are and what you do?...Why should they choose to support you over your competitors?

Chapter 1

The Power Of the Brand

DECISION TIME!

You're on summer vacation, driving to the beach.

You've been in the car for nearly three hours. The kids are in the back seat screaming that they're hungry and need to go to the bathroom. You look up ahead and see two options: one is McDonald's golden arches; the other is a sign for Frank's Home-Style Cooking.

Where do you stop? And why?

Even if you choose to bypass McDonald's, its brand—namely, what its golden arches signify—helps you make a quick and informed decision.

How?

Through branding—including marketing, advertising and word of mouth—McDonald's golden arches have come to symbolize inexpensive fast food served in a well-lit, family-friendly environment. Its uniformed staff may not drape napkins over their wrists, but the service is reasonable, and for the most part the restrooms are clean and safe. You may not be captivated by what's on the menu, but you know what you are going to get and what it is going to cost.

What do you know about Frank's Home-Style Cooking?

Now put yourself in the place of a funder who has dozens of applications on his or her desk, a tight deadline to meet and limited resources to allocate. Which organization is most likely to receive funding; one that the funder knows, trusts and values or a relatively unknown entity?

A SHORTCUT TO RECOGNITION

Branding represents a short cut, an instant recognition of what an organization—be it for-profit or not-for-profit—stands for. It is relationship-building that starts with a covenant, or promise, that an organization makes to its audiences: "If you buy our products or services, or align yourself with our organization, you can expect this."

> Your brand lets people recognize instantly what your organization stands for.

Think of Nike, IBM, the American Red Cross, the Salvation Army or any number of other well-branded companies and organizations. As soon as you see their logos or hear their names, you have an instant reaction.

Now think of your organization and its brand. When people see its name or logo, especially people you *want* to see it—namely potential customers, funders, partners or policy-makers—what images immediately pop into their minds, if any?

Do they truly understand who you are and what you do? Have you made it clear to them why they should buy your products or services, or align themselves with you in any meaningful way? Do they understand the impact you have in your community? In short, why should they choose to support you over your competitors?

ABOUT THIS BOOK

This book is intended for executive directors, board members and the communications, marketing and development staffs of small- to medium-size nonprofit organizations.

However, the principles of good branding are universal and apply to all businesses, organizations and government agencies with a need to get their messages out to their audiences.

> **The principles of good branding are universal. Therefore, regardless of whether your organization is a not-for-profit, for-profit or government agency, this book contains something for you.**

As you read through these pages you will notice that many examples and references are related to the community development corporation (CDC) portion of the nonprofit world, which primarily focuses on getting low- and moderate-income families into homes they can afford. That's because over the past several years I have spent a great deal of my time working with CDCs.

Regardless of the type of organization you work for, the ultimate goal of this book is to help you understand that branding is not the sole domain of large, well-funded corporations that can afford multimillion-dollar advertising budgets and celebrity endorsements. But that you, too, through efficient and cost-effective means, can raise the visibility and value—namely, the brand—of your organization in powerful and meaningful ways.

Branding for Success focuses on practical insights and hands-on exercises related to what I believe are the three most essential components of branding:

- How to define your brand

- How to promote your brand

- How to protect your brand

By its end you will have been given the opportunity to create a self-styled plan to incorporate critical branding elements into your everyday business activities.

The fact is the number of nonprofits in the United States has exploded in the last several decades to an estimated 1.6 million—with thousands more coming into existence every year.

It should come as no surprise, therefore, that whether you are seeking to attract customers, funders, board members, employees, volunteers or partners, competition is fierce. And given the pervasiveness of today's media, including the Internet, the public has access to more information than ever to make informed choices about which organizations to support.

Branding is a tool to help you break through the clutter, and to identify your company or organization as one that is worth supporting and doing business with.

> **A brand that is well defined, well promoted and well protected is priceless.**

And *Branding for Success* is a roadmap for helping you do just that.

What is a Brand, Anyway?

*Like it or not, you already own a brand.
Anyone who has ever come into contact
with your organization has an impression of
who you are and what you do....But is it the
impression you want them to have?*

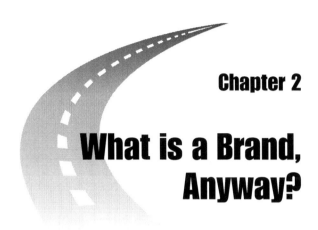

Chapter 2

What is a Brand, Anyway?

THE PURPOSE OF A BRAND

Your brand is the ultimate expression of everything your organization is and does. It is the overall image or impression people have of your work, your reputation, your staff, your leadership, your organization's culture and core values, as well as its programs, services and products.

> **Marketing and advertising are about selling your products and services. Branding is about selling everything associated with your organization.**

In a grocery or clothing store, a brand is what draws customers to one product over another. A good brand creates a positive feeling, image, understanding, recognition, or sense of connection between the consumer and the product.

In the case of McDonald's, the brand conveys quick food at affordable prices. With Nike, the brand communicates a can-do, confident, successful attitude to its sports-minded audience. In the case of nonprofits, the brand is why funders, partners, or the public, in general, opt to support one organization over another.

A QUICK REALITY CHECK

Answer the following:

	True	False
• Our organization already has a brand.	❏	❏
• Our leadership understands the value of raising our organization's brand visibility among customers, donors, funders, partners, referral agencies and policy-makers.	❏	❏
• Our community has a clear understanding of "who we are" and "what we do"—as well as "why" and "how" we do it.	❏	❏
• The people and organizations we seek as funders and partners trust and respect what we say and do, and therefore, want to help, support and do business with us.	❏	❏
• Everyone from our board members to our executive and support staff understands what it means to "live" our brand—namely how to protect and keep our good name strong, safe and positive.	❏	❏

If your organization operates like the majority of nonprofits and small businesses there is a high probability you answered "false" to one if not all of the above. Many small organizations simply rely on their reputations for their success. Small- to medium-size nonprofits, in particular, have traditionally depended heavily on governments and foundations for their support and have not felt the need to concern themselves too much with raising brand visibility to increase their revenue streams.

CHANGING TIMES

But times have changed.

In our post September 11th world, government deficits at the national, state and local levels are soaring, thus resulting in a decline in government funding for housing and other human services—at a time, we are all painfully aware, when the demand for these services is dramatically increasing.

In addition, a wary stock market has forced philanthropic foundations to cut back on both the number and dollar amounts of their grants. Years of mergers and acquisitions within the corporate sector continue to reduce the number of potential funding sources. In many cases, the loss of a job or job insecurity has curtailed family spending and giving. And large-scale international disasters, like the 2004 tsunami in Asia, are redirecting donations that would otherwise go to domestic nonprofits.

In short, competition for dwindling resources is becoming more ferocious than ever. It's not enough to simply be good at what you do—you need to differentiate your organization and business from the competition. The fact is that people align themselves, support

> It's not enough to simply be good at what you do—you need to differentiate your organization from the competition. The fact is people align themselves, support and do business with organizations they know, trust and feel good about.

and do business with organizations they know, trust and feel good about.

And that's where branding comes in.

"THE BEST KEPT SECRET IN TOWN"

Be honest. Have you ever said or thought that "Our organization is one of the best kept secrets in town"? Plenty of executive directors, development professionals and other nonprofit leaders—at both the local *and* national levels—use exactly those words when referring to the good work their organizations perform. For some it has become a mantra.

For whatever reasons, the nonprofit sector has a tendency to undersell itself. It is either too proud or too humble, too understaffed, too involved in providing services or too overwhelmed by day-to-day survival to promote its true value to the people and communities it serves.

> **Donors want to see the results of their giving. They want more accountability and clearer outcomes; they want to give to organizations that speak their language; and they want the satisfaction that comes with knowing that their contributions are making a difference. To attract these donors, nonprofits need to tell their "stories" more actively and more effectively.**

Fortunately, the idea of branding is beginning to take hold within the sector. As nonprofits continue to feel increased competition for dollars—as well as for qualified staff, board members and volunteers—they are beginning to understand how branding can help them bring clarity to their advocacy roles and help strengthen their voices on behalf of those they serve.

Many nonprofit leaders who possess a basic understanding of how branding works think it's a great idea. However, for whatever reasc they have yet to clearly define or effectively promote a brand for their organizations. Alternately, many others still hold to the notion that "branding would move us too much from our not-for-profit values and principles; it would make us look too much like the for-profit sector."

That may be so, but we have entered a new era of philanthropic giving. Donors are no longer content to write checks simply to appease their consciences or get fundraisers off their backs.

Donors, especially high-end donors, now want to see the results of their giving. They want more transparency in organizational accountability and clearer outcomes; they want to give to organizations that speak their language; and they want the satisfaction that comes with knowing that their contributions are making a difference.

For nonprofits this means that their organizations need to be more actively and effectively engaged when it comes to telling their stories. They need to brand for success.

A CASE STUDY

A couple of years ago, I was having lunch with the executive director of a small community development corporation (CDC) and her board chair in a little café when she turned to me and matter-of-factly said, "You know, last year we were responsible for more than $6 million worth of economic activity

> **To most people in the community, this organization was just another nonprofit out there doing whatever it is nonprofits do.**

in this community, and most of it went to small businesses in the construction, retail and appliance industries."

I was stunned. That was a big number for the size of the small town the CDC was serving, especially given the fact that the community was in the midst of a recession.

"Who else, outside of your organization, is aware of that fact?" I asked.

The executive director and board chair looked at one another, and almost in unison said, "No one."

They obviously had no strategy for getting this kind of valuable information about their organization out to those with a need to know—including civic organizations like the local Chamber of Commerce, as well as potential funders. To most people in the community, some of whom may have directly or indirectly benefited from this CDC's efforts, it was just another nonprofit out there doing whatever it is nonprofits do. Instead of effectively cultivating goodwill and new revenue streams by going to the public with its success stories, this particular organization was content with its legitimate right to be one of the best kept secrets in town.

> **One way to better understand the value of your organization is to ask yourself, "What would our community look like, or how would it be different, if we didn't exist?"**

AN OLD CONCEPT WITH A NEW TWIST

Branding is an old concept adapted to fit our modern times. Ranchers for hundreds of years have been branding cattle to distinguish them from other herds.

> **Ranchers for hundreds of years have been branding cattle to distinguish them from other herds.**

Today, savvy organizations and businesses use the ever-present media and sophisticated word-of-mouth campaigns to build brands around who they are and what they do to distinguish themselves from their competition.

A GOOD BRAND REQUIRES TLC:
A TRUE STORY

My family has been going to the same dental practice for years. It may be one of the most expensive in town. This is a group of professionals who pride themselves on acquiring and knowing how to employ the latest in dental technology (most of which seems focused on pain reduction, which I think is the reason my wife likes it so much). The waiting area and examination rooms are attractively appointed; all the dentists and hygienists are extremely skilled and personable; and the receptionists are as warm and friendly as can be. Even the Musak playing softly in the background is agreeable.

In short, this practice is not simply about dentistry. This is a business that over time has distinguished itself by building a solid brand image around the ultimate in professionalism and state-of-the-art dental technology delivered in a peaceful, soothing customer-friendly environment. These attributes are the covenant, or promise, that the practice has made to its clients—and it nearly succeeds in making "going to the dentist" seem like a pleasant experience. And as my wife likes to say, "I don't mind paying a premium for that."

> **This is a business that over time has distinguished itself by building a solid brand image around the ultimate in professionalism and state-of-the-art dental technology delivered in a peaceful, soothing customer-friendly environment.**

As a result of this kind of appreciation for and loyalty to the brand, she and I never hesitate to recommend the practice whenever someone asks us if we know of a good dentist in town.

Imagine my wife's shock when one day she calls to make an appointment and is treated differently than she expects from this business.

"I can't believe it," my wife said to me in exasperation after she hung up the phone. "I've never been treated like that before by anyone in that office."

Now, my wife isn't someone who often complains about being mistreated. On the contrary, she has worked in the education field for years, mostly around teenagers, and subsequently has a high level of tolerance for what others might consider less than civil behavior. But after getting off of this particular phone call she was visibly upset.

"The receptionist was simply rude to me for no reason," she huffed.

"Maybe she's just having a bad day," I consoled.

"Maybe so," replied my wife, "but I don't think Dr. G would be happy if he knew that one of his patients was treated this way."

And therein lies the rub. The brand image that Dr. G and his associates take such pride in promoting, at least in my wife's eyes, was ever so slightly tarnished by that one bad phone call experience with a receptionist.

Now, does this mean that our family will no longer have our teeth cleaned, drilled, extracted or capped by Dr. G's practice in the future? No. But there is now a small chink in the brand, and I can assure you that should another incident like this occur, my wife will, at the very least, be less inclined to recommend the practice to others.

THE MORAL TO THE STORY

When we speak about creating or defining a brand for a business or organization, we are not simply talking about developing an attractive logo and catchy tagline that can be slapped on to stationery, signage, brochures and the like, and, voila, we have a brand.

On the contrary, we are recognizing that a brand is fluid and dynamic, and everything that an organization and its staff do is a reflection on its brand. The quality of its products and

> **Successful branding is the art of managing the image you want your target audiences to have of you.**

services, the way those products and services are delivered, the way staff treat and relate to customers, funders, partners and each other, and how people perceive who you are and what you do are all part of the brand experience. Just ask my wife!

LIKE IT OR NOT, YOU ALREADY OWN A BRAND

That's right. Anyone who has ever come into contact with your organization—its products, programs, services or staff—or has heard of you through other sources, already has an impression of who you are and what you do. The questions you need to ask are:

- Is the impression people have of our organization accurate and complete?

- More importantly, is it the impression we want them to have?

To answer these questions may require a bit of research on your part, which we will get to in a moment. But your ultimate job is to define a brand that honestly reflects your organization's business and core values.

For example, you might want your brand to position your organization as:

- A producer of quality products and services.

- A good steward of funds.

- Caring and responsive to the needs of its customers.

- A reliable, trustworthy business partner.

This would be a powerful brand to own. Yet, in the same way that branding is not simply putting your logo and tagline on everything you own and calling it your brand, it is just as important to remember that your brand is more than setting forth a laundry list of desirable impressions about your organization.

Branding is all about fulfillment, about keeping the promises or commitments your brand messages make to your audiences. (In

Chapter 6, *Protecting Your Brand*, we will talk about what happens, even to the best brands, when a business or organization fails to keep its brand promises.)

NO QUICK FIXES

There are no quick fixes to creating a solid brand image. It requires time, coordination, discipline and some resources. But it's not as difficult as oral surgery, either.

If branding is the art of managing your image and if perception is reality, then it's your job, through branding, to ensure that the perceptions your audiences have of your organization are honest and

Branding entails organizing and formalizing the way you communicate to your target audiences, both internal and external.

accurate—and the impressions you want them to have.

MAKE BRANDING PART OF YOUR STRATEGIC PLAN

A strategic plan is a tool used by organizations to help strengthen their management and performance levels. In its simplest form a strategic plan combines a long-term vision of what an organization aspires to accomplish—as well as clarity about its organizational identity—with short-term goals and objectives that move the organization toward its vision. In other words, "Where do we want to be two to five years from now, and what is it going to take to get us there?"

Strategic planning and defining a brand have a lot in common. Both essentially require an organization to take an intensively honest and introspective look at itself and ask: What are our core values? What do we seek to accomplish as a result of our work? How do we approach our work, and what unique value do we offer to the community and those we serve?

For organizations contemplating undergoing a strategic planning process for the first time, or updating an existing strategic plan, it is the perfect opportunity to also seriously consider your brand image. At a minimum you will make the most use of limited resources and time by gathering information useful for both strategic planning *and* branding.

HOW BRANDING SUPPORTS THE GOALS AND OBJECTIVES OF A STRATEGIC PLAN

A good brand will:

- Enable you to manage your organization's image, namely how you want the public and especially your target audiences to view you.

- Raise your visibility and value among your targeted audiences.

- Establish your case for fundraising. (It's not surprising that branding and fundraising go hand in hand. People will financially support you only if they know, trust and value what you do.)

- Open up the possibility of new revenue streams.

- Enable you to vie more competitively for dwindling resources.

- Enhance your ability to serve as an effective advocate for your constituents.

Internally, a good brand also can motivate and inspire your workforce, both paid and volunteer. Think of some of the jobs you have held and the organizations and companies you have worked for in the past. Which ones did you feel best about?

> If a good strategic plan is a good _management_ tool then it follows that good branding serves as a good _messaging_ tool to help management achieve its stated goals and objectives.

People tend to take greater pride and are more productive in their work when it is clear to them what their organization is and does and the role they play in achieving its goals and objectives. Subsequently, a good, well-defined brand will help:

- Attract higher-quality board members, employees and volunteers.

- Focus and facilitate your fundraising efforts.

- Improve morale within your current workforce.

- Assist in employee retention.

It is hard to imagine a strategic plan that does not aspire to guide an organization in accomplishing many, if not all, of the above objectives.

In short, if a good strategic plan is a good _management_ tool then it follows that good branding serves as a good _messaging_ tool to help management achieve its stated goals and objectives.

Defining Your Brand

A brand needs to answer the questions: Who are we?…What do we do?… How do we do it?… And why should anyone care?

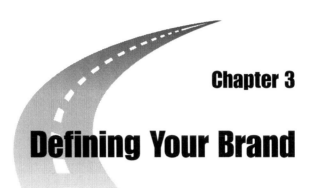

Chapter 3

Defining Your Brand

SORT OUT COMPETING INTERESTS

For many organizations, identifying their brand may not be an easy task.

Often competing interests need to be sorted out and an introspective process needs to take place before an organization can reach consensus on a brand identity.

People at all levels of the organization—not just senior management—will need to come together, discuss and arrive at consensus on many issues related to how the organization wants to talk about itself, namely the brand messages it would like to convey to targeted audiences.

> **When it comes to defining your brand, you need to listen to everyone in your organization.**

The fact is that when it comes to defining your brand, you need to listen to everyone in your organization—including your direct service providers and the people who answer your phones. After all, it is at their level that the rubber truly hits the road (see Chapter 4, *Promoting Your Brand*).

You will find that the time, effort and resources invested in defining your brand are well worth the results—namely, a brand identity that everyone in your organization can claim ownership to and promote with pride and confidence.

WHO ARE WE?... WHAT DO WE DO?... HOW DO WE DO IT?... AND WHY SHOULD ANYONE CARE?

A successful brand tells a positive, personally relevant story about its organization that focuses not only on the way business is conducted, but also on the outcomes that result from the organization's work.

Essentially, a brand needs to answer the following questions:

- Who are we?

- What do we do?

- How do we do it?

- And why should anyone care?

Many corporations and large nonprofit organizations have the financial wherewithal to spend tens of thousands, if not millions of dollars to answer these questions. Lots of time, resources and energy are devoted to researching their target audiences, both internal and external, to learn as much about these audiences as they possibly can so that they can build brands—i.e. create logos, messages, products and services, and a corporate culture—that their audiences will appreciate, understand and support.

Unfortunately, most small- to medium-size nonprofits and small businesses don't have that financial luxury.

One cost-effective way of laying a successful foundation for gaining consensus around a brand is to conduct an internal analysis of your organization's strengths, weaknesses, opportunities and threats with what is commonly referred to as a SWOT analysis.

This introspective analysis is a useful tool to help you come to a better understanding—and internal consensus—on the opportunities and obstacles you might face in defining and promoting your brand, as well as the kinds of messages you may want your brand to convey about your organization.

> **To be successful, a SWOT analysis—of Strengths, Weaknesses, Opportunities and Threats—must be conducted honestly and openly, and with the full support and involvement of your leadership.**

HANDLING OPPOSITION

Clearly defining your brand may suggest important ways for your organization to change, both in the way it perceives and talks about itself, as well as how some internal processes may need to be altered so that clear, consistent messages can be conveyed to your audiences.

But some people simply don't like change, no matter how good the reasons for it may be. Therefore, don't be surprised to find opposition within your ranks, even at the highest levels.

Those who resist change are best managed by gradually giving them responsibility—or ownership—for some meaningful phase of the branding process. You will be pleased how, after a while, many will convert into your most avid brand supporters.

While we're on the topic of change, the case also can be made that the majority of nonprofits are constantly seeking ways to offer more and improved services to help more people. However, you cannot expect different outcomes — including growth — without taking different approaches. In other words, you can't expect to help more people with better services tomorrow if you don't change what you are doing today.

Branding is an approach that can help you develop the kind of recognition and resources you need to make the kinds of changes that will help your organization grow, prosper and better serve its constituent audiences.

GETTING STARTED

What follows is an easy five-step process for an organization to begin defining its brand. In outlining this process, I am calling on years of experience helping nonprofits improve their communications. However, nothing here is written in stone. What is offered is a simple, practical, cost-effective roadmap for defining your brand, a foundation on which you can build as you become more familiar and comfortable with the branding process.

> Remember, when it comes to brainstorming, there are no right or wrong answers or ideas. Whoever is overseeing the SWOT analysis process must ensure that all participants be allowed to express their thoughts openly and freely, without restraint or ridicule.

Step 1—Conduct your SWOT analysis

Conduct your SWOT analysis by bringing leadership and staff to the table to brainstorm for organizational Strengths, Weaknesses, Opportunities and Threats.

Participation in the SWOT analysis process should include at least one representative from every level of your organization, including your board, executive staff, as well as management, operations and support staff.

Depending on how deeply people get into this process, it may require more than one session. In fact, to help people maintain their focus, you might want to carve out time for four sessions, one for each of the SWOT categories below.

Start by creating four (4) worksheets and use the "suggested questions" beneath each worksheet heading on the following pages to help get you started on your SWOT analysis.

Some questions can be used for multiple SWOT categories. For example, depending on your organization, questions related to your board, or staff or the economic landscape in your community may reflect an organizational strength or weakness, an opportunity or threat.

DO NOT limit the SWOT analysis group to the suggested questions. They need to take the analysis wherever they feel it needs to go.

Through the SWOT analysis you will more than likely come up with more information than you think you could possibly use. But every item on your SWOT sheets tells you something about your organization, including to whom you should target your brand messages, things you may need to do to address some of your organizational weaknesses, what kinds of politically related issues you may need to be sensitive to as you go about defining and promoting your brand, and more.

If you can afford it, consider using a professional facilitator familiar with both your organization and the concept of branding to help you work through your SWOT analysis. If cost is an issue, check with your board members, supporters, funders and local service organizations. They may be able to offer or guide you to *pro bono* facilitation services.

SWOT WORKSHEET #1: STRENGTHS

What are our organization's internal strengths, and how can we best use those strengths to better position our organization in the eyes of the public, especially with partners, clients, funders, policy-makers, etc.?

Suggested questions to start with:

- What do we do best?

- What are we best known for with respect to our products and/or service delivery?

- What is our commitment to our clients? What value do they receive from our organization?

- How do we think people view the quality of our organization, including what they think of our staff and the services we provide?

- How do we want our target audiences to view us? What attributes do we want to highlight and convey through our brand?

- What distinguishes us from our competition? And what value can we place on those distinctions?

- Who do we especially want to know these things, namely, who are our primary audiences? Our secondary audiences? Our third-tier audiences?

SWOT WORKSHEET #2: WEAKNESSES

What are our internal weaknesses as an organization, and what do we need to do to address them?

Suggested questions to start with:

- In what ways do we have trouble clearly explaining to people outside our field what our organization does?

- In what ways, if any, have our clients been unhappy or dissatisfied with our work? And how do they demonstrate their displeasure?

- What is the makeup of our current board and what kind of support or resistance can we expect with respect to strengthening our image?

- How much does our board know about branding, and how effective will members be in promoting and protecting our brand?

- What about our staff? What is their overall morale like toward their work and our organization, and how receptive would they be to working more openly and closely with each other to actively promote a consistent and unified brand image?

- How is our organizational culture perceived, both internally and externally? What can we do to improve on it?

SWOT WORKSHEET #3: OPPORTUNITIES

What external opportunities exist for strengthening our image or brand?

Suggested questions to start with:

- Can we identify an expanding market for our products and services?

- Does the community we serve value the types of services we provide?

- Can we identify new or additional funding sources to support what we do?

- What is the current economic landscape of our community? Is it prospering? If so, which sectors and how can we tap into them?

- Are there new opportunities for collaboration with other organizations that can help us better achieve our mission and make better use of our resources?

- What opportunities exist for strengthening our board, our staff, our relationships with other organizations, and the community in general?

SWOT WORKSHEET #4: THREATS

Are there external forces facing our organization that may threaten our brand image?

Suggested questions to start with:

- Are there any external factors that would prohibit our organization from more aggressively promoting our brand? (i.e., funders, regulators, constituents, partners who might resist; local politics that may need to be considered?)

- Who are our competitors? How much do we know about who they are and what they do? Are we competing with them for the same customers and funding sources?

- Is our organization's current name a barrier to a clear, unified, understandable brand? Should we consider changing our name? What would be the repercussions?

- Will people in our organization and those who financially support us view the resources required to strengthen our brand as a cost or as an investment in the long-term viability and strength of our organization?

- Are we planning on changing the direction of what we do anytime soon, and what impact will that have on our brand?

SWOT ANALYSIS RESULTS

Our 3 Greatest Strengths	Implications for Branding
1.	
2.	
3.	
Our 3 Most Important Weaknesses	Implications for Branding
1.	
2.	
3.	
Our 3 Biggest Opportunities	Implications for Branding
1.	
2.	
3.	
Our 3 Most Important Threats	Implications for Branding
1.	
2.	
3.	

Step 2—Review your SWOT analysis for brand messaging opportunities

Once you have completed your SWOT analysis, and everyone's views and ideas have been considered, review it carefully and begin selecting those things that you believe best reflect how you would like to position your organization and its brand. What have you unearthed in the course of the process that best reflects who you are, what you do, how you do it, and why anyone should care?

> When analyzing and discussing the results of your internal SWOT analysis, rather than focus your efforts on resolving <u>differences</u> when working with colleagues about SWOT outcomes, concentrate on areas and issues where people <u>share common ground.</u> Then build on that common ground to begin identifying your brand.

Competing interests within an organization often are difficult to resolve internally and may require an objective third party, or consultant, to help bring the group to consensus.

A good consultant can bring a certain weight to sensitive internal issues and sometimes facilitate change more effectively. It is often easier for an outsider to do and say things related to critical issues than it is for those inside the organization. This is especially true if major differences of opinion exist among key players.

Step 3—Determine what messages your audiences want or need to hear

There's an old saying in the communication field that states, "It's not how a message is delivered, but rather how it is received that makes all the difference."

Put another way, what you might want to say about your organization—the messages you want your brand to convey—may not necessarily be the messages your audiences want or need to hear.

Let's use the affordable housing component of the nonprofit sector as an example.

> **What you might want to say about your organization may not necessarily be the messages your audiences want or need to hear.**

For decades, community development corporations (CDCs) have been relying on the message that they are in the business of providing affordable housing to needy low- and moderate-income families, many of whom spend as much as 50% or more of their incomes on housing costs. Certainly, this is a worthy and deserving cause that should resonate with most fair-minded people.

Research, however, suggests otherwise. It indicates that the public is not always interested in CDCs providing housing to needy people, especially when such housing may be in, or close by, their neighborhoods or communities and may be unattractive or poorly maintained, or draw crime and lower property values.

People appear to be more receptive to the notion of affordable housing, however, when they believe that such housing will have a positive impact on a wider mix of constituencies, especially children and the elderly, as well as on the community in general. "In some communities," according to a recent survey report, "this may take the form of messages about…tax benefits, or preserving a local downtown, or reducing traffic."

In other words, to be successful in their brand messaging, CDCs, in general, will need to rethink how they communicate about what they do, which may entail broadening their messages to include the larger impact of their work in the communities they serve.

> **When developing brand messages, think about the community you serve. What specifically does it want to know about your work?**

Broad-based national studies such as the one cited above are excellent resources to help guide smaller organizations that could not possibly fund such large-scale research.

But what about your local community? What specifically does it want to know about your work?

Again, this is a component of the branding process that large organizations spend lots of money to research. If you have the resources, you might want to consider conducting formal focus groups to gauge the appropriate branding messages for each of your community audiences, including clients, funders, partners and policy-makers.

However, there are far less costly ways to get reasonable readings on how your audiences feel about your organization and what they would like to know about you—namely, who you are and what you do.

An executive director of a relatively large, well-known national nonprofit, for example, wanted to learn what others thought of her organization's name. In lieu of expensive focus groups, she conducted, on her own and over the course of about a year, an informal survey of every nonprofit and corporate leader she ran into at meetings, conferences, business lunches, and so forth. She was told by the majority of those she asked that "We like what you do, but your organization's name just doesn't work for us". This eventually led to her organization successfully rebranding itself under a new name.

The above executive director went about conducting her survey by verbally asking people who were familiar with her organization what they thought. This proved to be highly effective.

For best results, surveys should be kept short, simple, and to the point.

You can also survey funders and partners through printed surveys (see *"Sample Survey"* at the end of this chapter), which can be distributed by mail or completed over the Internet via email. Clients and customers also can often be surveyed right at your place of business.

When surveying your audiences, ask questions that would give you a better understanding of:

- How they currently perceive your organization?

- What more they would like to know about who you are and what you do?

- What key words come to them when they think about your organization, its work, its relationship to clients, partners, funders, and the community, in general?

- What kinds of messages they think your brand needs to convey?

The overwhelming majority will give you their honest opinions.

Another option for getting answers to the questions above is by conducting small, "informal" focus groups consisting of representatives from each of your key audiences. These can be done in your meeting room during business hours or in the evening. If you don't have a meeting room, secure an appropriate space to conduct the event. Often churches, libraries or local government service centers will provide such space for free.

The point is to bring these folks together in a comfortable, relaxed setting where they can freely and confidentially discuss your organization and its relationship to them, their respective organizations and the community at large.

Step 4—Create a "messaging package"

Once you have completed both your internal and external research and come to consensus on what you believe your brand should convey, begin creating a messaging package. The package should contain:

A "messaging package" is simply a compilation of the core messages you want your brand to convey. Its purpose is to help you stay on message whenever you communicate information about your organization.

- A tagline

- Mission statement

- Positioning statement

- Supporting statements

- Logo

Tagline

A tagline is a catchy, quick-identifying reference, usually no more than five to seven words in length. It is designed to capture the imagination and interest of your target audiences.

Examples of some effective and well-recognized taglines include:

- General Electric — *We bring good things to life*

- Nike — *Just Do it*

- American Red Cross — *Together we can save a life*

- National Endowment for the Arts — *A great nation deserves great art*

What do these taglines have in common?

In addition to being catchy and easy to remember, they all elicit an emotion or an energy that people tend to gravitate to naturally, something they can associate with that is positive and good.

Your tagline should be incorporated into all your materials, including signage, business stationery, banners, media materials, website, etc.

Keep in mind, however, that like logos (see *"Logo"* below),

In many instances, your tagline is a stand-alone communication that may be the first message new audiences receive about your organization. They may come across it on your business card, stationery or signage. Therefore, at the very least, a good tagline needs to send a positive message that cannot be interpreted as inappropriate or offensive to any audience.

taglines are only a small piece of the messaging package. A handful of words can only convey so much.

Mission and positioning statements

Most organizations already have mission statements. A mission statement describes your reason for being and points to your core goals and objectives. It basically answers the question: Why do we exist? In other words, "What difference do we make in the world?"

For example:

> *"The mission of XYZ is to provide safe, quality housing that low- and moderate-income families can afford."*

A positioning statement builds upon the mission statement by summarizing how you go about achieving your goals. For example:

> *"XYZ is a leading community-based nonprofit organization that works in partnership with others to provide homes that low- and moderate-income families can afford, and acts as a catalyst for inspiring local grassroots leadership and community development. Last year, we helped 216 families purchase their first homes and were responsible for $6 million of local economic activity. We are efficient and caring in our work, good stewards of financial resources, and easy to do business with. Join us in helping to open doors for others."*

> **A positioning statement is often referred to as an "elevator speech," something that can be delivered quickly to a stranger who knows nothing about your organization.**

A positioning statement is often referred to as an "elevator speech," something that can be delivered quickly to a stranger who knows nothing about your organization. Therefore, keep it short, simple and compelling.

The purpose of your positioning statement is not to educate people about every program or service your organization offers. But rather it should be compelling enough to interest them in your overall mission, to get them to care enough about what you do—and your importance to the community—so that they will want to learn more.

Supporting statements

Supporting statements are just that—they support the brand by providing additional facts about your organization to targeted audiences.

For example, supporting statements may address:

- Your core values.

- The range of programs and services you offer.

- How long your organization has been in existence.

- The trust and reliability you have built over the years.

- How effectively and innovatively you go about your work.

- Who currently supports you and how.

- How the local economic impact you generate affects local jobs, businesses, etc.

- What impact your work has on the larger community, which might mean safer, healthier, more attractive communities that everyone can appreciate; better schools because home-owning parents are more involved in their kids' educations; "smart growth" development that brings people closer to places where they work and eases traffic congestion, etc.

Think of supporting statements as talking points to be included in your speeches, presentations, many of your printed materials, on your website, and elsewhere.

Logo

> **If you already have a logo, it should be used consistently on your letterhead, annual reports, brochures, website, signage, etc.**

In addition to verbal and written messages, good branding also includes giving all of your materials a consistent look and style so that people can identify immediately with your organization.

And your logo is the cornerstone to that look and style. (Think of McDonald's golden arches, Nike's swoosh, and the Red Cross's, well, red cross.)

Whatever you decide upon for a logo, it should be attractive and representative of your organization and its brand.

Also, when considering its design and colors, think about the various ways you may use it and how difficult or expensive it may be to reproduce. Consider proportions, as well. A detailed logo that looks great on a large banner may not reproduce well when it is reduced small enough to fit on a business card. Also, how will it look in black and white, faxed, enlarged or reduced.

What follows is a quick and easy exercise you can do right in your office. Place on a conference table or large desk five to seven printed materials your organization has produced over the last couple of years, including annual reports, brochures, flyers, report covers, press releases, video covers, etc.

Ask yourself:

- Do these materials all look like they come from the same organization?

- Is our logo used on all of these materials? If so, is it being used uniformly and consistently?

- Are these materials attractive?

- Are they legible, and is there enough white space to make them reader friendly?

- Do they reflect our brand?

- If I were to receive any of these items in the mail or notice one on a table or in a brochure rack, would I be compelled to pick it up and read it?

If your answer is "No" to the above, it's time to find a new designer—or at least give the current designer better instructions on how to promote your brand.

Again, remember that a logo is only a small part of your brand. By using it often and consistently on all your materials it will go a long way to raising your visibility. But it's your messaging package and your people (which we will talk about in the next chapter) that convey the true value of your organization by telling people more precisely who you are, what you do, how you do it—and why they should care.

Step 5—Go back to your focus groups

Before going public with your newly created brand messages and/ or logo, go back to your focus groups—not necessarily the same people, but certainly the same audiences—and ask them if what you have arrived at as a description of your brand resonates with them. Remember, through decisions they make about whether or not to support your organization, they are the ones who will ultimately decide whether your brand is successful or not.

You may be wondering why the need to go through this extra step. "Haven't we already surveyed these folks, and haven't they presumably told us what they want to know about us?" you might ask. Yes, they have. But in the process of creating your messaging package, you interpreted much of what they had to say into your own words. And words are very powerful things that mean different things to different people.

> **Words that organizations felt described themselves ideally, were interpreted extremely differently when re-tested in focus groups.**

For example, words that organizations felt described themselves ideally to the public, when re-tested in focus groups—made up of audiences that these words were designed to reach and influence—were interpreted extremely differently.

Let's take the word "partnership." It's a good, simple word used often to describe relationships. It implies affiliation, collaboration, and alliance, all of which form positive brand images. But in certain circles partnership is a strong word that has legal implications that other organizations, or funders may not buy into when it comes to relating to your organization.

Here's another example of the power of words and language: Remember earlier in this chapter when we referred to the research indicating that the public isn't necessarily enamored that community development corporations are providing "affordable housing" to needy people?

The term "affordable housing" has taken on a negative connotation over the years. It tends to be associated with housing for the poor or those lowest on the income scale, when in reality many people currently locked out of the housing market are teachers, police officers, service- and retail-industry employees, healthcare workers, including nurses, and others who provide indispensable services to our communities. Many of these working families represent a population segment that many CDCs are attempting to place into good, safe "affordable housing."

Now imagine how differently the public might perceive the work of CDCs if these organizations positioned themselves as providers of "homes that people can afford" rather than "affordable housing." The two phrases conjure up entirely different images.

> **Language is a powerful tool. It forms our images, thoughts, opinions and actions. Therefore, when defining your brand, choose your words wisely.**

"Homes that people can afford" is something most of us can relate to, especially those of us fortunate enough to have bought our homes five or ten years ago. Given how much housing has appreciated in value in recent years, we can easily relate to how much more difficult it would be, even for us, to buy the homes we reside in today.

In short, the phrase "homes that people can afford" gives a sense of communal purpose and understanding; "affordable housing" conjures up images of "those *other* people."

The lesson? Language is a powerful tool. It forms our images, thoughts, opinions and actions. Therefore, when defining your brand, choose your words wisely. If resources allow, consider using a professional writer to help create your messaging package.

SAMPLE CUSTOMER SURVEY

1. How did you learn about us?

Brochure ❑   Advertisement ❑   Flyer ❑   Word of mouth ❑
Other (explain) _____

2. What programs or services of ours did you use? [*Note: Examples relate to possible CDC-type programs/services*]

Financial literacy ❑   Pre-purchase education ❑
Post-purchase education ❑   Home maintenance ❑
Other(s) _____

3. Did you know about all the services we offer prior to coming to our organization? Yes ❑   No ❑

4. How would you rate the quality of the program(s) or service(s) you used?

   1   2   3   4   5   6   7   8   9   10
   poor   excellent

5. How would you rate the professionalism of our staff?

   1   2   3   4   5   6   7   8   9   10
   poor   excellent

6. How would you rate your overall experience with our organization?

    1   2   3   4   5   6   7   8   9   10

    poor   excellent

7. In your opinion, how well-known is our organization in the community?

    1   2   3   4   5   6   7   8   9   10

    not very well-known   very well-known

8. Would you recommend our organization to your family/friends?

    Yes ❑   No ❑

9. What words would you use to describe our organization?
For example: caring/ uncaring, responsive/unresponsive, knowledgeable/unknowledgeable, etc.

_____

_____

_____

Please write any additional comments you may have on the back of this survey.

Thank you!

Promoting Your Brand

Some of the best branding opportunities are through word of mouth that starts with your employees.

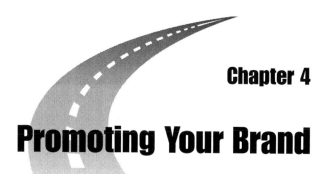

Chapter 4

Promoting Your Brand

MAXIMIZING OPPORTUNITIES

An excellent branding opportunity is about to present itself to one of your staff who is attending a party unrelated to your organization's business. She is among a group of strangers. Not surprisingly, everyone is fetching for conversation. The inevitable ice-breaker is posed: *"So, what do you do for a living?"* The ensuing conversation can either be a boost to your organization's brand or a squandered opportunity.

Conversation #1

> *"I work for a local community development corporation,"*
> *she replies.*

> *"Oh? What does it do?"*

> *"We do lots of things. It's really hard to explain."*

End of conversation.

Or

Conversation #2

"I work for a local community development corporation. We're a nonprofit that helps low- and moderate-income families buy homes they can afford."

"Oh, really?"

"Yes, if they have financial problems, we provide them with free debt counseling, and then suggest ways that will help them save money for their down payment. In some cases, we even offer them grants."

"No kidding."

"No, and before they buy a home, we provide a pre-purchase course so they'll know what to expect when they begin dealing with real estate agents, mortgage brokers, housing inspectors and attorneys, as well as what will be required of them at closing."

"I wish I'd known more about that stuff before I bought my first home."

"Lots of people do. We also offer a post-purchase course and a course on home maintenance so they'll know what it takes to take care of and stay in their new home."

"And all this for free!?"

"Yes, or for a very nominal cost for some of the services. You see, we're funded mostly by foundation, corporate, and government grants, as well as gifts from individuals. But we're always looking for additional revenue so we can help more people. We use some of our funds to purchase and refurbish old housing stock in the community. As

bad as the economy was around here last year, we were responsible for more than $6 million worth of local economic activity, most of it going to small businesses."

"I'm impressed. I've got some friends and family members who might be able to use your services. I also know someone who might be able to help you out financially. Does your organization accept donations?"

> The employee in Conversation #1 has a job. The employee in Conversation #2 has a mission—to be a Brand Ambassador for your organization.

BEGIN BRANDING FROM THE INSIDE OUT

The above two conversations provide an excellent argument for why it's important to begin your branding from the inside out.

Many small- and medium-size nonprofits and businesses often shy away from branding because they think it requires large advertising budgets, which most can't afford. Others believe that once they have developed a logo and have agreed on their brand identity, their next step is to go public with their brand messages.

What they often fail to realize is that some of their best branding opportunities are through word of mouth that starts with their employees, volunteers, donors, and service recipients. If they are passionate believers in the work that you do, are valued as partners in achieving your mission, and well versed in the

> Consider this: The founders of both Amazon.com and Google relied exclusively on word of mouth to get their companies off the ground.

messages you are seeking to send to your audiences, then these people are the best Brand Ambassadors you could hope for.

WHEN TREATED WITH RESPECT
PEOPLE WILL SAY THE DARNDEST THINGS

Here's a story for you: Several years ago, after a Chicago Bulls' basketball game in which mega athlete Michael "Air" Jordan scored a mind-boggling 69 points, the team's locker room was jammed with reporters. Most of them huddled around Jordan, hanging on his every word. One reporter, realizing he wasn't going to be able to get close to the Superstar, noticed one of Jordan's teammates, a rookie, sitting on a bench away from the crowd. He recalled Jordan having patted the rookie on the back and speaking words of encouragement to him as they made their way into the locker room.

The reporter also remembered that the rookie had only scored one point during the game, a seemingly inconsequential foul shot in the face of Jordan's amazing scoring binge.

Thinking he would take a different approach to the post-game story, the reporter sat down beside the lone rookie and asked: "What are your thoughts on this game, and what do you think about the fact that Michael Jordan scored 69 points while you scored only one?"

The rookie took a towel, wiped the sweat from his face, looked up at the reporter, and proudly said with a big grin: "I'll always remember this as the game Michael Jordan and I teamed up to score 70 points."

Whether the story is true or not, it makes an excellent point: Make people feel that they are part of your team and it's amazing what they will say about you. And by people, I mean everyone from your board members to the people who answer your phones.

ONE OPPORTUNITY
TO MAKE A GOOD FIRST IMPRESSION

It is more than likely that the overwhelming majority of first contacts with your organization are not through board members or your executive director, but rather over the telephone. If the person answering that phone is less than friendly and cannot answer the caller's questions, or worse yet, gives them the runaround, that caller will hang up with a far different impression of your organization than if he or she had interacted with someone who was knowledgeable, courteous and helpful. (Think back to Chapter 2 and recall my wife's experience over the phone with the receptionist at the dentist's office.)

Creating good Brand Ambassadors takes time and resources, but not as much as you might think. Here are a few simple suggestions to get you started:

• Train your staff, board, and volunteers in the principles of good branding and what it means to be a good Brand Ambassador for your organization. For example, incorporate Brand Ambassadorship in your new-hire orientations and as a regular part of your staff meeting agenda. Your entire staff should know what your brand is and the messages you want your brand to convey to your audiences.

• Have them share their experiences "living the brand" (see next chapter). In this way they are both learning from each other and reinforcing the brand at the same time. Think of all the key brand messages that were conveyed about the organization in

Conversation #2 at the beginning of this chapter, including what the organization is, what it does, who it does it for, what impact it has on the people served, as well as the community in general—not to mention the impression the knowledgeable Brand Ambassador left on the listener about the quality of the organization's staff.

- Create a one- or two-page summary of the most frequently asked questions (FAQs) you get about your organization and make sure everyone in your organization not only gets a copy, but knows the answers to those questions.

- To keep the message in front of them, give board members, staff, volunteers, donors and service recipients "Post-it" notepads and coffee mugs with your organization's tagline on them. You can even create computer screen-savers for your staff that contain your key branding messages.

- Include "Brand Ambassadorship" as part of your employees' performance reviews. How well do they know the brand messages you want to convey? How many opportunities have they taken to convey those messages in speeches and presentations they may give during the year or at informal gatherings they may attend? How well do they reflect the values and ethics of your organization's brand, both on and off the job?

- Recognize and reward staff for being good Ambassadors. Recognition can be as simple as calling a staff member or volunteer into your office and thanking them for their efforts. Or you can acknowledge your best Brand Ambassadors at a special awards dinner or luncheon, and make a point of letting everyone present know the positive role these individuals have played in promoting your brand.

Be creative, and never underestimate the power of saying "thank-you." A little acknowledgement and recognition often go a long way. And it doesn't cost very much, either.

CREATE BRAND AMBASSADORS... AND BRAND ADVOCATES WILL FOLLOW

Let's take the concept of Brand Ambassador one step further: It follows that good Brand Ambassadors create good Brand Advocates.

Go back to Conversation #2. The messages given to the person by your Brand Ambassador won't necessarily stop with him or her. There is a very good chance that when the name of your organization comes up again in conversation elsewhere, he or she will recall the positive messages articulated by your Ambassador and pass them on to others, in effect becoming an Advocate for your brand. Think of this Brand Ambassador/Brand Advocate process as a tree that continues to branch out and bear fruit.

> Your brand is only as good as the people who represent it and live it day-in and day-out. It is they who embody its absolute value. And it is with them that you should start your branding efforts.

The fact is a solid brand that is well represented by staff allows your partners, customers, and funders to tell your story to others with confidence and in good faith.

BUILDING YOUR BRAND IN THE COMMUNITY

Once you've done a thorough job of educating everyone internally about your brand and the important roles each plays in promoting it, it is now time to take it to the public. And becoming more actively involved in your community is an excellent way to get started.

Active and frequent community involvement provides cost-effective opportunities for people in other organizations to learn first-hand who you are, what you do and why they should care. It raises your brand profile in the community, and gives you the chance to collaborate with other organizations in achieving your goals.

Remember, branding is very much about building positive relationships. And there is no better way to build these relationships than through community engagement.

Your board, staff and volunteers need to get out from behind their desks and actively work to make your organization a major player in community affairs. Here are some suggestions for building your brand through community engagement:

- Create points of entry. That is, invite prospective donors, community leaders, media representatives and others to your organization so that they can see for themselves first-hand what it is you do, as well as get answers to any questions they might have about your organization.

- Seek out every opportunity to network and work with other businesses, organizations and community leaders.

- Encourage your staff to attend civic organization meetings to answer questions about your organization. These are great opportunities to explain to community leaders who you are, what you do, how you do it—and why they should care!

- Share resources and information with other community organizations.

- Demonstrate your willingness to work with others to help resolve community issues by volunteering to get involved in local task force efforts.

- Be sensitive to the cultural make-up of your community. If the neighborhoods you are working in are multilingual, be sure you have someone on your staff who can communicate fluently with the people living and working in those areas. It's difficult to build a relationship or promote a brand when a language barrier exists.

- Take every opportunity to promote your brand messages to family, friends, business associates and people you meet while traveling. These are all easy, cost-effective ways to create Brand Advocates (see above).

Increasing your brand visibility in the community will serve a multitude of purposes, including helping you attract new revenue streams, as well as recruit better qualified and motivated employees and volunteers. It will also facilitate partnerships and collaborations with other organizations.

TURN YOUR STAFF INTO MEDIA MAVENS

You may not be able to afford to place many ads in magazines or newspapers, or on radio or TV. But make no mistake about it; the media are an important component to the success of your brand image. The visibility and credibility of your organization rest largely on the way you work with individual reporters and editors.

It is a fact that the media are always looking for "experts" to quote in their stories. Make your organization one of those reliable sources of expert information that the media can count on—especially when they are on tight deadlines. You'll make friends forever!

> **Every opportunity to be cited by the media is a branding opportunity—namely an opportunity to raise the visibility and value of your organization.**

Every opportunity to be cited by the media is a branding opportunity—namely an opportunity to raise the visibility and value of your organization. Just make sure you are being cited for all the right reasons. (We will talk about "living your brand" in the next chapter.)

What follows are some suggestions to help your organization work successfully with the media:

- Establish personal relationships with your local media assignment editors and reporters. Call them to introduce yourself and your organization. Offer to have lunch together or to meet with them to discuss possible story ideas that relate to your work. Being on a friendly "first-name basis" with these people can be priceless.

- Start by focusing on the smaller media outlets. If your organization is in a large metropolitan area, you may find it difficult to get stories into the larger newspapers or TV outlets. But even the largest of metropolitan areas—including New York, Washington, DC, Los Angeles, Chicago and others—are serviced by a myriad of smaller community newspapers and local cable TV stations that are often hungry for good, local news stories. Work to make your organization a source for that news.

- Make your staff reliable sources of industry-specific information to the media. This will encourage news outlets to call on them whenever they are seeking information related to your field of work or business.

- If you can afford it, provide your board members and staff with media training.

- Anything you can do to help the media meet their deadlines will definitely place your organization in their good graces. Make sure, therefore, that media questions are answered promptly, fully, accurately and courteously. If you don't know the answer to a particular question, either find it quickly or refer the reporter to another helpful source. Don't fake it!

- Seize upon opportunities. If you know the media are about to do a story related to your work, don't wait to be called by them. Make yourself available by calling and letting them know how you can add value to their story.

- Whenever possible, make the connection between your organization's local services and how they tie into current national or global issues and news.

- Don't hesitate to send the media a press release whenever you are about to launch a new initiative or program, or holding a special event. In short, keep the media informed of everything you do that demonstrates your value to the community.

Being responsive and helpful at all times, as well as recognizing the needs of the media in your community are cost-effective ways to help you elevate your brand image.

OTHER COST-EFFECTIVE WAYS TO PROMOTE YOUR BRAND

Websites

Your website should be a reflection of your brand. It is the perfect vehicle for promoting your logo and tagline, conveying your brand messages and telling your organization's story.

> **Your website should be a reflection of your brand.**

Make sure, however, that your site is maintained and updated regularly and is easy to navigate. There are few things more frustrating than to go to a website only to find out-dated information or, worse still, to have to navigate through a maze of menus and pages to find information you thought would be at your fingertips.

If you don't already have a website, seriously consider devoting the time, energy and resources to create one. A couple of good, cost-effective, on-line resources to help you get started include www.charityadvantage.com and techsoup.org.

Given the explosive growth of the Internet, and how widely used it has become as a source for all kinds of information—including researching the missions, services and quality of nonprofits—not having a website puts your organization at a distinct disadvantage.

Signage

Never underestimate the importance of putting up a good, effective sign.

Consider: A large nonprofit with several branch offices located in densely populated ethnic city neighborhoods has been serving these communities for nearly 30 years. Yet, many of the residents did not know the organization existed.

Focus groups revealed that the organization's signage was too small and in fierce competition with all the other signs displayed in the neighborhood by commercial businesses.

> Good branding is more than placing a sign outside your door. Good branding is making sure that the message on that sign is simple and clear, and that it succeeds in attracting the eyes of your target audience.

Those who did notice the organization's signs said they were not descriptive enough, meaning that the organization's name, alone on the sign, did not explain what kinds of services it offered.

Also, most people who saw the signs did not realize the organization was a nonprofit, but instead thought it was a government agency. Given that most people in the neighborhood were immigrants skeptical of government activity, few, if any, took the additional step of walking through the door to learn more.

Here's another true story about signage: A CDC developed a neighborhood of wonderfully designed single-family homes for moderate-income families located in a quiet but fairly well-traveled part of town. It was obviously a work of great love and pride. The CDC, however, had not bothered to post any signage that told who had created this wonderful enclave of attractive homes. When asked why not, the response was "signs are expensive." That may be the case, but had the CDC gone to the banks, architects, mortgage and real estate companies that helped to make the project possible, the likelihood is that these partners would have been more than happy to underwrite the cost of the signage, especially if their company names were included.

"Co-branding" opportunities such as the above are win-win for all concerned and are an excellent way to not only raise the visibility and value of your own brand in the community by identifying the work that you do; it also benefits the brands of partners and funders, as well. It's a chance for great community relationship-building.

"Company-wear"

Take a lesson from the sportswear industry and use "company-wear" to raise your brand visibility, whenever it's appropriate.

T-shirts with your organization's logo and tagline are great for handing out at picnics and special events. Many organizations also have attractive polo shirts with their logos stitched on them that are often appropriate for staff and others when "business casual" is called for. Such attire often initiates conversation and is a good entrée for telling your organization's story.

And there's just no end to other logo-bearing hand-outs like calendars, pencils and pens, refrigerator magnets, jar openers, and so forth. All of which are easy, inexpensive ways to promote your brand.

Whenever possible, get others to tell your story.

Testimonials

Personal testimonials carry powerful messages. Therefore, whenever possible, get people your organization has successfully served to tell their personal stories to others.

Testimonials, especially when accompanied by compelling photographs, can be used in all your printed materials, from brochures and flyers to annual reports and press releases. Be sure, however, that you receive written permission before using the names and photographs of those speaking on your behalf.

Also, consider inviting a client or customer who represents one of your success stories to join you when you speak to other organizations about your work. In a dignified setting and in their own words, let them express how their lives have been improved or even transformed as a result of your organization's programs, products and services.

Spokespersons

"Wouldn't it be great if we could just get so-and-so (insert the name of some high profile individual) to be our spokesperson?"

Whether they are large organizations seeking to raise their profiles on the national scene or regional or local organizations wanting to elevate their visibility state-wide or regionally, the topic of spokesperson seems to come up often. Today, "celebrities" of all kinds—including athletes, pop stars and retired public servants—are speaking on behalf of all sorts of organizations and causes.

Perhaps the most admired and referred to spokesperson in the nonprofit housing arena is former president Jimmy Carter

> Organizations that seek to have well-known people speak on their behalf need to understand that all of these speakers, regardless of who they are, come with liabilities as well as likeable, well-known faces—and some of these liabilities can take you totally by surprise.

who has become the national icon for Habitat for Humanity. A true believer in decent housing for all people, the former president and first lady raise the brand visibility of that organization every time they don a pair of overalls and wield a hammer on a Habitat for Humanity construction site.

However, there aren't many Jimmy and Rosalyn Carters out there. And organizations that seek to have well-known people speak on their behalf need to understand that all of these celebrity spokespersons, regardless of who they are, come with liabilities as well as likeable, well-known faces — and some of these liabilities can take you totally by surprise.

> You need to think about the availability of celebrities. Their time is often in high demand, which comes with serious scheduling challenges. How committed—and available —will they be when you need them?

Many of us are old enough to remember when the tall, handsome actor James Garner appeared on TV as spokesperson for the beef industry. This was at a time when conscientious consumers were eliminating red meat from their diets to lower their risk of heart disease. And there was Mr. Garner, with his rugged good looks, standing in front of a large outdoor grill somewhere on what appeared to be the Great Plains telling Americans about the virtues of a good, well-cooked steak.

Some of us may recall that Mr. Garner was released as spokesperson for the beef industry shortly after he suffered a heart attack. Although agents representing the actor at the time attributed the heart attack to Mr. Garner's long history of heavy smoking, it certainly didn't do much to dissuade the public of the association between red meat and heart disease.

This is not to say that seeking a spokesperson is something you should absolutely not consider. Rather, when selecting someone for the job, make sure you scrutinize wisely and are conscious of all the possible liabilities you may be taking on—including additional costs.

For example, "free" could end up being very expensive. Even if some of these celebrity-types agree to act as spokespeople on a *pro bono* basis, many will often demand first-class travel and room accommodations whenever they attend your meetings or conferences—a cost you might not have expected or can easily afford.

Protecting Your Brand

Many of the issues your organization grapples with on a daily basis, including economic, social and political, are for the most part out of your control. Protecting your brand—namely, living it well—is completely in your hands.

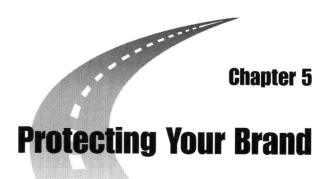

Chapter 5

Protecting Your Brand

GREAT BRANDS GONE BAD

If defining and promoting your brand is important, then living your brand is essential! This is especially true now, when public distrust of institutions of all kinds is high.

Arthur Andersen. Recall the name? For most of the 20th century Arthur Andersen was considered by many to be the platinum standard in corporate accounting. Its 28,000 U.S. employees served the accounting needs of 1,300 of America's most well-known public companies. By the first year of the 21st century, however, this once venerable 90-year-old company no longer existed under that once proud name.

Why?

Arthur Andersen failed to live up to its long tradition of integrity. As a result of avarice, poor leadership and mismanagement, the company began placing profits before protection of its brand and looked the other way as many of its multi-million dollar clients, including Enron, Worldcom and Global Crossing fudged their books.

In 2002, Arthur Andersen was convicted of obstruction of justice. Fortune 500 companies that once relied on Andersen for their auditing services dropped the company like a hot potato. It wasn't long afterwards that the company was forced to file for bankruptcy and soon ceased operations.

It should be noted that Enron, Worldcom and Global Crossing all suffered similar fates as a result of neglecting their brands and not living up to the covenants they had made with their audiences, including their employees, many of whom not only lost their jobs, but much of their life savings, as well.

NONPROFITS ARE NOT EXEMPT

For anyone who even remotely follows news of the nonprofit sector, it should come as no surprise that plenty of once-venerable nonprofit organizations have their own sad stories of brand neglect—and their disastrous consequences.

> **Over time your brand will turn perceptions into belief in the good work your organization performs. This in turn often translates into increased support—but only if you stay true to your brand.**

The fact is the public and media are merciless on organizations of all sizes, types and in all sectors of our society— including not-for-profits, for-profits, government agencies, even faith-based institutions— that fail to live up to their brands, meaning the attributes and values they publicly promote and espouse. And for many of these organizations, the consequences result in the negation of all they have invested in creating a good brand name.

Regardless of public or media impact, living your brand is simply the right thing to do.

What does it mean to live a brand?

IT ALL STARTS AT THE TOP

It all starts with moral, ethical — and, yes, compassionate, sensitive, and wise leadership (now when was the last time you saw any of those words on a job application or required as part of the criteria for board membership?) — and trickles down from there. Everyone in your organization — including board members — must know the value of your brand, what it represents, the important role he or she plays in protecting it — and especially what is at risk if the brand is not vigilantly maintained and protected.

Board leaders and staff must be made aware that they are Ambassadors of your brand in all that they say and do — both on and off the job. Board members need to govern well and wisely; executive directors must ensure that the organization's mission is carried out as effectively and efficiently as possible; and every staff member needs to be brand-wise, including courteous and responsive to all who walk through your doors, or otherwise make contact with your organization.

This can be accomplished through workshops, seminars or retreats, but most importantly through leadership by example.

The fact is that when it comes to living your brand, your

> **When it comes to living your brand, your people can either be your greatest asset or worst liability. Create an organizational cultural that gives them every opportunity to become the former.**

people can either be your greatest asset or worst liability. Continually work to seek ways to nurture an organizational cultural that gives them every opportunity to become the former. This will take an ongoing, organization-wide commitment, but it is essential to the protection and maintenance of your brand.

BE TRANSPARENT WITH YOUR FINANCES

This has evolved into a big issue. If the public and media learned anything from Watergate's Deep Throat it is to "follow the money." These days even a whiff of financial impropriety can create a public relations nightmare, as well as wreak havoc on an organization's hard-earned good name and brand. Therefore, be forthright and scrupulous in all your financial dealings, and transparent and diligent in your financial record keeping.

> **These days even a whiff of financial impropriety can create a public relations nightmare, as well as wreak havoc on an organization's hard-earned good name and brand.**

Remember, as a nonprofit the overwhelming majority of your funding comes from government agencies, philanthropic and corporate foundations, partners, and private individuals, all of whom deserve—and in most cases, are now demanding—accurate accounts of how their donations are being spent.

Also, poor bookkeeping is no excuse. Hire or retain a good accountant. It's well worth the investment.

Here are some tips to avoid misuse or misappropriation of organization funds:

- Conduct both internal and external financial audits at least once every fiscal year.

- Ask questions if things "don't add up"—regardless of who is doing the adding! Nothing less than your organization's reputation—if not very existence—may be at stake.

- Require two signatures on checks.

- Screen job applicants carefully, especially for any criminal records related to finances.

- Establish checks and balances for how funds are accounted for, including controls for company credit cards.

- Require periodic financial training for employees.

- Set down written procedures for all financial transactions.

LEGAL IS NOT THE LITMUS TEST
FOR DOING WHAT IS RIGHT

When accused of an impropriety in a public forum many organizations often take the fallback position that "what we did was not illegal." And that certainly may be the case. But more often than we would sometimes like to admit organizations, both for-profit and not-for-profit, alike, have seriously tarnished their brands—or worse—by misleading or misinforming the public.

> **The court of public opinion can be far harsher and more unforgiving than any legal proceedings held in a court of law.**

The caution: Regardless whether what you are doing is legal or not, trial in the court of public opinion can be far harsher and more unforgiving than any legal proceedings held in a court of law.

By far, the better litmus test regarding any policy or decision your organization makes is "If this were to appear on the evening news or front page of our city newspaper, how would the public, but especially our partners and funders, react?" There are plenty of examples of organizations that failed to use this litmus test—and the consequences they endured for not doing so.

EXPECTATIONS… EXPECTATIONS… EXPECTATIONS

In real estate, it's all about location, location, location. To sum up branding, it's all about expectations.

Your audiences have the right to expect that your organization will live up to its promises—or brand.

If your branding conveys positive messages about your programs, services, the way you treat customers or clients, your response time, your professionalism, knowledge, integrity, trustworthiness, or whatever, <u>you need to deliver on these promises</u>—or your brand will eventually suffer the consequences.

> **It is far easier to maintain a good brand by living up to what you publicly profess than to try to catch up to and rehabilitate one that has been tarnished through neglect.**

In our communications-saturated culture an organization's reputation travels faster, farther and in more ways than we can even imagine. Therefore, it is far easier to maintain a good brand by living up to what you publicly profess than to try to catch up to and rehabilitate one that has been tarnished through neglect.

Here's something else to consider: Many of the issues your nonprofit grapples with on a daily basis —i.e., economic, social, political—are for the most part out of your control. Living your brand, however, is completely in your hands.

All the more reason you should define, promote—and live it well!

Is There Ever Enough Information?!

The simple answer to this question is no.

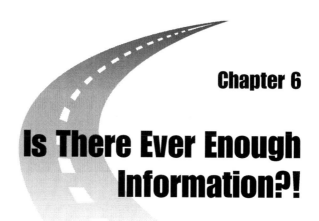

Chapter 6

Is There Ever Enough Information?!

MORE TIPS ON BRANDING

Focus on building value as well as visibility

Rationale: Developing an effective brand entails more than raising visibility through consistent and widespread use of a logo. Such efforts help to raise name recognition. However, an effective brand is built around a vision that reflects a positive identity, namely the "value" that the brand represents.

Again, when defining your brand, ask yourself: What do people think when they see our name or logo? Do they truly understand what we do and how we do it? Are we viewed as effective and trustworthy? What is it that we'd like people to feel when they see our brand or logo? What's in it for funders, companies, foundations, government entities, other nonprofit organizations and customers when they do business with us? In short, what's our identity? Why should anyone care about who we are and what we do?

View branding as a new way of doing business

Rationale: There are no quick fixes to creating a solid and successful brand image. On the contrary, it takes a great deal of introspection, time, effort, coordination and collaboration. And once you've defined your brand, it requires an ongoing effort to manage and maintain it. Therefore, consider brand maintenance an ongoing commitment that needs to be incorporated into your everyday business activities.

View branding as an organization-wide effort.

Rationale: Maintaining your brand should not be the responsibility of your organization's communication and/or marketing units, but rather must be viewed as an organization-wide effort in which every department and/or business unit understands that it has a role to play. Moreover, staff at all levels of the organization, regardless of job description, need to understand the goal to raise the visibility and value of your brand, and what part they are expected to play in achieving that goal (see *Educate your staff* below).

Keep the effort manageable, yet meaningful

Rationale: For staff in most small- to medium-size nonprofits just keeping up with day-to-day operations can be overwhelming. Consequently, keep branding efforts within the range of what is doable. For example, it doesn't take much in the way of time and resources to ensure clear, consistent messaging; to educate staff about the purpose and goals of branding; and to actively promote your brand through already scheduled public speaking engagements, events and publications.

Promote open communications and collaboration among staff.

Rationale: For any branding effort to succeed requires an atmosphere of open communications and collaboration among staff so that the organization can convey clear, consistent and accurate messages to target audiences. It also requires that everyone work toward common, rather than individual business unit goals. For the sake of uniformity and consistency of message, this more than likely will require some centralization of the message-creation and delivery process.

Educate your staff about brand expectations

Rationale: People can't represent or promote what they don't know or understand. Therefore, to build employee pride and understanding of your brand, incorporate a strong educational component into your branding effort. This should include time to understand the brand, as well as practice promoting the brand accurately and consistently, and thinking creatively about how they can integrate the brand into their role in the effort. Also, make supporting and promoting the brand part of your employees' overall performance reviews.

Lead by example

Rationale: Executive officers and board members need to champion your branding efforts. Leading by example demonstrates their commitment, and the importance they place behind these efforts. It reinforces the message to staff that "we are working together" to accomplish the goal of raising the visibility and value of our organization.

Be flexible and interactive

Rationale: Branding is a dynamic process. Maintain flexibility in your thinking and be open to suggestions from all parties for strengthening your brand. This will allow for better, more efficient use of resources as well as make for a more dynamic, interactive and collaborative process that takes advantage of branding opportunities as they arise.

Live your brand!

Rationale: Your brand reflects your promise to the public and your commitment to your staff and volunteers. Live that brand through all your words and deeds.

Also, your brand is only as good as the people who live it day to day. Staff and volunteers who are knowledgeable, who take pride in the brand, feel secure in their jobs, and are appreciated for the good work that they do make excellent Ambassadors for your brand.

About the Author

Larry Checco is President of Checco Communications. In his more than 25 years of communications experience, Larry has helped raise the brand visibility, fund raising capabilities, membership levels, and impact of some of the nation's most respected nonprofit organizations and government agencies, including the American Red Cross, Volunteers of America, United States Postal Inspection Service, National Institutes of Health and Neighborhood Reinvestment Corporation, now NeighborWorks America®.

Larry is a faculty member of the NeighborWorks® Training Institute. He also speaks, and conducts courses and workshops on branding.

Larry's articles on branding have been published by the National Housing Institute's *Shelterforce* magazine and appear on the websites of the Milano Graduate School of Management and Urban Policy, KnowledgePlex, and the Michigan State University library system.

Larry holds a degree in economics from Syracuse University, as well as an MA in Journalism and Public Affairs from American University.

He lives in Silver Spring, Maryland, with his wife, Laurie, and their two sons, Brian and Peter.

> **To learn more about this book, Larry, and how you can engage his consulting services, log on to www.checcocomm.net**

Acknowledgments

I would never have published this book without first having it pass the critical eyes of respected professionals, friends and family members who took the time to read it (some more than once, bless their hearts) and contributed their honest opinions, insights and information.

I'd like to start by thanking from the bottom of my heart my loving, and EXTREMELY patient wife, Laurie, who embodies a top-quality brand all her own. Many thanks to my good friend, Peter Shann Ford, who relentlessly encouraged me to write this book. It took a while, Peter, as do all good things. My thanks also to my very talented older son, Brian, whose original illustration inspired the cover for this book; to designer Felix Morales for his professionalism and fine work on the finished cover; and to my younger son, Peter, simply for being himself, a great kid.

Many lent me their eyes, ears, insights and inspiration during the time it took to get this book from my head into your hands. For their kind service—which was always offered in friendship and, in some cases, love—my thanks go to: Greg Alvord, Darrell Blandford, Dorothy Burochonock, Andy Burochonock, Steve Casady, Larry Checco, Sr., Lucy Checco, Christina Deady, Terence Feheley, Jeff Finn, Gail Fiorelli, Roland Fiorelli, Vera Hershey, Denice Rothman Hinden, Rich Innes, Paul Kealey, Ron Kerman, Jim King, Kathleen King, the ladies of Creative Wallworks (Kathy, Ellen & Barbara), Michael Lesparre, Mark Levine, Doug Lipton, Vicki Meade, Leslie O'Flahavan, Jake Plante, John Schall, Rob Sheehan, Carol Weisman, and Bob Zdenek.

I would also like to thank all those in the nonprofit world who have allowed me the privilege of working with them over the past 20-plus years or so of my career. Many of our mutual learning experiences and best practices regarding communications and branding are reflected in this book.

ISBN 1-41205249-1

Made in the USA
Lexington, KY
02 June 2010